# OF SUCH IS THE KINGDOM

## Object Sermons for Children

# ROBERT S. COOMBS AND IRIS PERRY

**BAKER BOOK HOUSE**

Grand Rapids, Michigan 49516

# OF SUCH IS THE KINGDOM

"Suffer the little children to come unto me,
and forbid them not:
for of such is the kingdom of God."
Mark 10:14

# Contents

8

# Acknowledgments

We are especially grateful to the children, young and old, of West Hills Baptist Church, Knoxville, Tennessee. Their eager acceptance and participation in the delivery of the children's sermons have been a continuous source of inspiration.

We also thank our very supportive and encouraging spouses, Janet Coombs and Carl Perry.

Many thanks to Amanda White for her long hours of typing and willing spirit of cooperation.

# Preface

Including a children's sermon as part of the worship service will add an extremely worthwhile and meaningful dimension to worship. Not only will the children feel that they have an important and vital place in the service, but the adults will also gain new insights to simple and yet profound truths.

A few guidelines are noteworthy regarding the development and delivery of a good children's sermon. Please consider the following suggestions:

1. If possible, have a designated area where you may sit and allow the children to gather around you. This provides the opportunity for closeness, eye-to-eye contact, and comfortable dialogue.
2. Begin each children's sermon in the same manner. This will allow each child to know what to expect and thus should prove relaxing. For example, I begin with a cheerful "Good Morning." The children have become accustomed to this and respond with a hearty "Good Morning" of their own.
3. A good children's sermon, like all good sermons, has *one* point and *one* point only. Many children's sermons suffer greatly because the minister seeks to make more than one point.
4. The children are the intended audience of the sermon. Therefore keep your one point simple and easy

to understand for the group you are addressing. (The adults will still benefit greatly from the simple truth expressed!)

5. Make your point in two to three minutes. Since a child's attention span is relatively short, even the very best sermon can be ruined by the failure to keep it brief.

6. Encourage interaction. The richest joy of this special time of worship will be the response of the children in your group. The opportunity to participate speaks directly to a child's worth. The feeling of self-worth and importance given to a child in this setting may well carry into adulthood.

7. Enjoy yourself. Preparation and delivery of a good children's sermon will bring such a worthwhile variety of results, they could well become a book in their own right.

# 1

# Unearned Love

**Text:** "For by grace you have been saved through faith; and this is not your own doing, it is the gift of God—not because of works, lest any man should boast" (Eph. 2:8–9).

**Object:** Quarter

**Theme:** God's love is unconditionally free.

Today I have a quarter with me which, of course, is worth twenty-five cents. When I was your age, I was given an allowance of twenty-five cents per week. I earned the quarter by performing various chores, such as washing dishes, making my bed, cleaning my room, taking out the trash, and working in the yard during the summer months. Of course, that was some time ago. I am really more interested in some of the ways you can earn money today. [Allow time for children to give examples.]

Who would like to have this quarter? [Give the quarter to the first child who raises his/her hand.] Some of you may have thought I would ask you to perform a task in order to earn this quarter. No, today this quarter is free. In fact, all you had to do was come up and get it, as (name) _____ just did.

Almost everything in life is earned, but there are a few precious things that are unconditionally free. The most wonderful gift in life, God's love, is absolutely free. Unlike a quarter that must be earned by working for it, God's love is given unconditionally, like the quarter I just gave to (name)

————. All you have to do is receive it. Let's thank God for his free gift of love.

*Thank you, God, for giving us your love unconditionally. Amen.*

# 2

# Blueprint for Living

**Text:** "For he has made known to us in all wisdom and insight the mystery of his will, according to his purpose which he set forth in Christ as a plan for the fulness of time, to unite all things in him, things in heaven and things on earth" (Eph. 1:9–10).

**Object:** Architectural blueprint

**Theme:** God has a wonderful plan for our lives.

Whenever you go for a ride in your parents' car through the city or your neighborhood, you will probably see some people busily building a new house, a store, a restaurant, or some other sort of building.

Suppose you want to build a building. What are some of the supplies you might need in order to build? [Children's answers will include items such as hammers, nails, bricks, wood, etc.] If I were to go out and buy the things you just mentioned, how would I know the way to fit everything together to make a building? [Children may have difficulty answering this question. After adequate time is allowed, give the answer.]

I need to have a plan. A plan for a building is called a blueprint. If you look closely at this blueprint, you will see that it is actually a picture or chart of everything that goes into a building. Doors, walls, windows, rooms, and hallways are all carefully drawn on this blueprint so that they will be built in the right place. If we had followed these plans, we would be sure to end up with a beautiful building. Without the blueprint, however, we would end up with a real mess: windows would be in the wrong place and doors would open backwards.

Just as we have plans to build homes and churches, we also have plans for our lives. God has given us the plans through Jesus' life and the teachings in the Bible. He has shown us how to build, and if we follow his blueprint, we can build beautiful lives. Without God's plan, however, our lives will end up in an awful mess.

So remember, to build a good and useful and beautiful building, we need to follow plans like these. To build good and useful and beautiful people, we need to follow God's plan for our lives.

*Dear God, thank you for giving us a blueprint, a plan for our lives. Help us to always follow your plan. Amen.*

# 3

# **Measuring God's Love**

**Text:** "For God so loved the world that he gave his only Son, that whoever believes in him should not perish but have eternal life" (John 3:16).

**Object:** Yardstick

**Theme:** God's love is so great that it cannot be measured.

Most of you know the object in my hand is used for measuring. It is called a _____ [yardstick]. It will measure thirty-six inches, or three feet. If I were to measure the width of this room, it would probably be seventy feet or more wide. What else can be measured with my yardstick? [Allow adequate time for the children to respond.] Yes, you can measure how tall you are. [Choose a child and measure.] Why, you are thirty-five inches, a little less than a yard. And you can measure how deep the water is in a swimming pool. If you are a good swimmer, you can go into the water four or five feet deep. How long is a football field? It is one hundred yards long. We would need to put 100 yardsticks in a straight line with the edges touching, to measure the field. So you see, we can measure how wide something is, how high or how tall, how deep and how long, can't we?

There is one thing that cannot be measured. We cannot measure how much God loves us. His love is so big, so wide, so long, and so deep that it has no end. In fact, he loves us so much that he gave his only Son so that we could live forever. John 3:16 is a verse from the Bible that tells us this. It begins, "For God so loved the world." Let's say this verse together. Perhaps the adults will join in with us. "For God so loved the world that he gave his only Son, that whoever believes in him should not perish but have eternal life."

*Dear God, thank you for loving us so much and for sending your Son to show us how to live forever. Amen.*

# 4

# Hide and Seek

**Text:** "For nothing is hid that shall not be made manifest, nor anything secret that shall not be known and come to light" (Luke 8:17).

**Object:** Game of Hide and Seek

**Theme:** Attempting to play Hide and Seek with God is no fun.

How many of you enjoy playing games? [Every child should enthusiastically respond to this question.] Good, this morning we are going to play a game. Raise your hands if you have ever played Hide and Seek. Great, it looks like everybody has played before. Have you ever played Hide and Seek in a church service? No? Would you like to play? This is really a great place for this game. There are plenty of excellent hiding places—behind the pews, in the choir loft, or even in the very back of the church.

I will close my eyes very tight and count to ten. All of you find a place to hide. [Your congregation should love this as children scurry in all directions. If you feel this game would be too disruptive, you may simply discuss how the game is played.] One, two, three, four, five, six, seven, eight, nine, ten. Ready or not, here I come! [Seek out several children, and then ask the rest to come out from their hiding places and return to their seats.] All of you found good places to hide. In fact, it might have taken the rest of the service just to find you!

Did you enjoy playing this game? [Allow the children to respond.] Yes, playing Hide and Seek can be a lot of fun. Did you know that sometimes as children grow up, they try to play this game with God? Some people think they can run and hide from God just like you ran and hid from me. They look for just the right place to hide, a real neat hiding place where God won't see them or know what they are doing. Of course, we cannot really hide from God like we hide from each other. He always knows where we are and what we are doing.

Playing Hide and Seek with our friends may be fun, but attempting to play Hide and Seek with God is never fun. That's because when we are trying to hide from God we cannot be happy. In fact, the very happiest we can possibly be is when we are not trying to hide from God, but when we are very, very close to God.

*Dear God, help us to realize that we can never hide from you, and help us to walk closely in your presence every day. Amen.*

# 5

# A Strong Foundation

**Text:** "For no other foundation can any one lay than that which is laid, which is Jesus Christ" (1 Cor. 3:11).

**Object:** Concrete building block

**Theme:** We must build our lives on the strong foundation, Jesus Christ.

I wonder if anyone can tell me what I have with me this morning? [Allow the children time to respond.] What a smart group! You're right—this is a concrete block. That must have been a pretty easy question. Does anyone think he or she can lift this block? Perhaps that is not so easy! [Allow a couple of children to attempt to lift the block.]

Can you think of some ways a big heavy concrete block like this is used? [Some of the older children should know the answer to this question.] That's correct—to provide a foundation for a building such as your home or our church. Why do you suppose the blocks used to build foundations are so strong and heavy? [Allow children to explain why strong blocks are necessary.] Exactly. A block must be very strong if it is going to support a heavy building. A block made of cardboard or plastic would soon be crushed under the weight of the building. So something strong like this concrete block must be used so that the building will not fall down. We can see how very important it is to build a building on a strong foundation.

As important as it is to use very strong blocks for building, Jesus knew it was even more important to build our lives on something very strong. So Jesus said we should build our lives on a rock. What he meant was that we should build our lives on a strong foundation, like this heavy block. The strongest and best material we can build our lives on is a commitment to Jesus Christ. Just like this strong and beautiful church was built on blocks like this one, our lives, if they are built on Jesus, become strong and beautiful.

The way we build our lives on Jesus is first by accepting Christ as our Savior: that is our strong foundation. And then we continue to build our lives by following his teaching and example, his actions and speech, his kindness and love.

Let's ask God to help us remember to always build our lives on the strong foundation of Jesus.

*Dear God, thank you for the strength we find in our lives when we build them on the foundation of Jesus Christ. Amen.*

# 6

# Empty Lives

**Text:** "May the God of hope fill you with all joy and peace in
believing, so that by the power of the Holy Spirit you may
abound in hope" (Rom. 15:13).

**Object:** Clock with inner works removed

**Theme:** Jesus fills our minds and hearts with all that is
needed for living.

This morning I really need your help. I'm having a problem with this clock. It simply refuses to run. I hate to throw
the clock away. You can see it looks as good as new, but a
clock that never tells the right time is not useful. Perhaps
some of you could give helpful suggestions as to what is
needed to return this clock to proper working order. [Al-
low time for children to offer suggestions. If someone sug-
gests winding the mainspring, use this suggestion. If not,
make the suggestion yourself.]

Winding the clock is a great idea. I'll see if that will help.
There is nothing back here to turn; the winding stem is
gone! I'm afraid we have some real problems here. I guess
the only alternative now is to investigate further by taking
this clock apart. [Remove the exterior casing of the clock.]

No wonder this clock does not run—all the inner parts
are missing! This clock cannot possibly work right, because it is empty! Funny, the clock appeared fine on the
outside. It looked like it would work properly. But no mat-

ter how nice it looks on the outside, this clock will never run because it is empty on the inside.

Sometimes you and I can be a lot like this clock. From the outside we may present a fine appearance, but on the inside we are rather empty. Unfortunately, when we are empty on the inside, we become as useless as this clock. Emptiness from within may even cause more damage to us than it does to a clock. A poor attitude, an absence of love in our hearts, and a lack of concern for others are all signs of emptiness.

As Jesus comes into our lives, he fills our hearts and minds, making all parts of our lives work properly, and we become as useful as a finely tuned clock.

*Dear God, fill us with your Spirit and your love so that we can live abundant and useful lives. Amen.*

# 7

# Books and Covers

**Text:** "Do not judge by appearances, but judge with right judgment" (John 7:24).

**Object:** Children's book and book cover from another book

**Theme:** We may be fooled by someone's outward appearance, but we will not be fooled if we seek to understand his/her heart.

As you can see, this morning I have brought a rather large book with me. I thought perhaps this book would be of special interest to all of you. Can anybody tell me the name of this book? I know we have some pretty good readers in this group. [Allow adequate time for a response.] That's right—the name of this book is *All About Roses*. What do you suppose is inside this book? [Children will quickly respond in accordance with what they believe the book to be about—a book about roses, how they grow, and how to care for them.] That makes sense to me. A book all about roses surely ought to tell how to grow and care for roses.

Let's take a peek inside and see if you are right. This book is not about roses! In fact, I do not see any flowers in here at all. All I see are pictures of pets! Why, this book is not about taking care of roses, it's about taking care of pets! I do not understand. On the outside the book plainly says, *All About Roses*, but on the inside the book is clearly about the care of pets. I wonder what the problem is?

25

[Some of the children may have caught on and will identify the problem.]

What's that—the wrong cover? [Remove the cover.] You are right! This book has the wrong cover. All along we believed this book was about roses because the cover said it was. Now, by taking off the cover, we know for sure that this book is really about pets and not about roses. Looking only at the cover of this book and trying to guess what was on the inside fooled us all.

People can be a lot like books with covers. Sometimes you may think you know all about a person because of his or her appearance—how that person looks on the outside. But you may find after you come to really know the person you were all wrong. That is why God always looks on the inside, or into your heart. He knows that what is on the outside may not really show what is on the inside.

Next time you are thinking about a friend, remember this book with the wrong cover. Thinking of this book will help you to remember it is what is on the inside, not the outside, that really counts.

*Dear God, help us to look at the inside of people and not to judge them by their outward appearances. Amen.*

# 8

# Answering the Alarm

**Text:** "Therefore encourage one another and build one another up, just as you are doing" (1 Thess. 5:11).

**Object:** Smoke alarm

**Theme:** We can be good friends by detecting when others have special needs during times of trouble.

This morning I have a rather strange-looking object with me. We do not often see this object unless we are looking up at the ceiling. I suppose most of us have one in our own homes. Can anyone tell me what this is? [Allow adequate time for a response.]

That's right! This is a smoke alarm. How is a smoke alarm used? [Allow adequate time for a response.] This is a smart group. You are right again. A smoke alarm tells us when there is a fire. Suppose you and your family were all asleep one night, and a fire broke out in your home. Before long you would hear this sound. [Push the test button to demonstrate the sound.] As soon as you heard this loud noise, you and your family would know that there was something wrong. Then you would have time to get out of the house before anybody would be hurt by the fire. So as you can see, a smoke alarm is great to have because it can be a big help in warning us about something terribly wrong, like a fire in our house.

Did you know people also give warning signals when they have a problem or feel like something is wrong? Of course they do not make a loud noise like this smoke alarm. But if we watch closely, we might see a sad face or even someone crying because of a problem. That is when it is important for each of us to see these warning signals and try to help. We can help by saying a kind word or by lending a helping hand to make a person feel better.

This smoke detector is a great friend because it is always watching to tell us when our home is having a problem. We, too, can be good friends by watching and helping others when they are having problems.

*Dear God, may each of us be a special friend by watching and helping others who have problems. Amen.*

# 9

# Taming the Tongue

**Text:** "For we all make many mistakes, and if any one makes no mistakes in what he says he is a perfect man, able to bridle the whole body also. If we put bits into the mouths of horses that they may obey us, we guide their whole bodies" (James 3:2–3).

**Object:** Horse bridle

**Theme:** We must control our tongues.

I have an object with me that perhaps a few of you might recognize. Notice that it has several leather straps that are very, very strong and also a heavy metal piece. Can anyone tell me what it is? [Allow the children to respond.] Right, this is a horse bridle.

Does the bridle go on the back of the horse, on his tail, or on one of his feet? [Children will point out that the bridle is worn on the horse's head.] You all are too smart for me. The bridle does fit on the horse's head like this. [Demonstrate.] Why do you suppose we would put a bridle on a horse's head? [The children will explain that a bridle is necessary to control where the horse goes.] Without a good bridle like this, it would be pretty hard to make a horse turn the way we would like him to go. But with this bridle a horse will turn left or right or even back up. Of course, the best thing about a bridle is that it can make the horse stop! Imagine we are riding across a field in a full gallop—that is, as fast as a horse can run—and we see that

29

the horse is running toward a row of trees. That is when it is a good idea to stop. All we have to do is pull back on these straps, and the horse will stop. The reason the horse stops is this little U shape on the metal piece. Whenever we pull on the straps, this little U-shaped piece pushes on the tongue of the horse. No matter how big or how strong the horse may be, when this piece presses on his tongue, he will stop. So you see, the whole horse is controlled by his little tongue.

James, a New Testament writer, once said that each of us is controlled by our tongue. Even though our tongue is very small, it really controls our whole body. That is because every word we say with our tongue tells something about who we are.

As important as it is to control the tongue of a horse to get him to stop, it is even more important to control your own tongue. An uncontrolled tongue that says only bad words is like a horse running wild—it can cause a lot of damage. But a controlled tongue that says only good and kind words can do a lot of good, just like a horse that is under control.

Let's ask God to help control our tongue to say only what is good.

*Dear God, help us to control our tongues so that we say only good and kind things. Amen.*

# 10

# Impossible Possibilities

**Text:** "For truly, I say to you, if you have faith as a grain of mustard seed, you will say to this mountain, 'Move from here to there,' and it will move; and nothing will be impossible to you" (Matt. 17:20b–21).

**Object:** Potato and straw

**Theme:** Faith enables us to face all of life's challenges.

This morning I have an ordinary Idaho potato, one I took out of the potato sack before coming to church. Potatoes such as this one can be cooked in a variety of ways. Perhaps you can suggest a few. [Children will respond with several suggestions, such as baked potatoes, french fries, creamed potatoes, and so on.] I'm afraid your delicious suggestions are making me a little hungry. However, my intention this morning is not to eat this potato. Instead, I plan to put this straw through the center of it. You do believe I can put the straw through the potato, don't you? [Some of the children will readily respond yes, while others will doubt the possibility.] I see some of you believe I can and some do not. Perhaps I will choose a few volunteers to try for themselves. Okay, (name) _____, (name) _____, and (name) _____, each of you may take a turn trying to put the straw through the middle of the raw potato. [Children will make interesting comments about the

31

impossibility of this task.] You all seem to agree that it is impossible to put the straw through the potato. I believe you have even convinced your friends of the impossibility.

It does *look* impossible, doesn't it? [In one hand place the potato between the thumb and forefinger, and with the other hand grasp the straw, putting your thumb over the top of the straw in order to trap air. Then forcefully and quickly shove the straw through the center of the potato. Although this is fairly simple to do, a few practice sessions are in order!] Even though it looks impossible, it really can be done.

Many times you may think you just can't do something. The task seems too hard for you or the problem too big for you to handle. In those moments, the Bible teaches us that faith can make what appears to be impossible, possible. In fact, a life lived by faith can equip us to face and overcome all of life's problems, both small and large.

*Dear God, help us to believe that we can always solve our problems and difficulties with your help, and help us to always depend on you. Amen.*

# 11

## Important Days

**Text:** "This is the day which the LORD has made; let us rejoice and be glad in it" (Ps. 118:24).

**Object:** Calendar

**Theme:** Each day of our lives is a precious gift from God.

I believe that each one of you will be familiar with the object I have this morning. That's right—this is a month-by-month calendar of the year, with a pretty picture for each month.

As I was looking through this calendar the other day, I began to wonder about the most important days of the year. Of course, the first one to come to mind was _____ [your birthday]. I guess everyone knows the importance of that day. No? Why, that's my birthday! What do you think are the most important days of the year? [Children will respond with answers such as Christmas, Easter, Thanksgiving, their birthdays, and so on.] I can see you all have different opinions as to which day is the most important.

Although we think that some days (such as Christmas and Easter) are important, we should always keep in mind that life itself is a gift from God. Therefore, every single day is an important day. In fact, every day God gives us should be considered a special gift from God. Perhaps if we were to see each day in this manner, we would be more likely to seek to please God every day.

33

Next time you are looking at a calendar, remember that there really are no ordinary days. Each day is an important and special gift from God.

*Dear God, thank you for each and every day that you give us. Help us to make each day full and meaningful. Amen.*

# **12**

# God's Medicine

**Text:** "What then shall we say to this? If God is for us, who is against us? He who did not spare his own Son but gave him up for us all, will he not also give us all things with him?" (Rom. 8:31–32).

**Object:** Thermometer

**Theme:** God provides healing medicine for emotional and spiritual needs.

Seeing a thermometer like this one may bring back some unpleasant memories—memories of days spent in bed rather than playing outdoors with your friends, and memories, too, of feeling sick all over.

When you are feeling sick, does your mother reach into the medicine cabinet and bring out the thermometer? [Allow an opportunity for response.] What does a thermometer tell your mother? [Allow an opportunity for response.] Right, the temperature of your body. If your temperature is above 98.6 degrees, chances are there is a good reason why you are feeling sick. You may have a sore throat, an ear infection, a virus, or the flu. If your temperature remains above normal for a long period of time, your mother may even decide you need to visit the doctor's office. The doctor or nurse will probably ask you to take some medicine to help return your temperature to normal and make you well again.

Isn't it wonderful to have so many things to help keep our physical bodies healthy? Thermometers, medicine, mothers, nurses, and doctors work together to assure the best possible protection for our bodies.

Sometimes we have problems that are not like sore throats or ear infections, problems such as worry, sadness, or disappointment. We need help for these problems also, but we need something more than a thermometer or medicine can provide. These are problems we take to God. He is always ready to help, no matter what the problem may be. We only have to ask him when we pray, and he provides the proper medicine.

So next time you are feeling sick, and the thermometer indicates you have a high temperature, take the advice of your mother so that you will recover quickly. And when you are troubled with sadness, loneliness, or disappointment, remember to turn to God, who provides medicine for your greatest needs.

*Dear God, we thank you for helping us when we are in trouble and when we are sad or disappointed. Help us to always depend on you when we are in need. Amen.*

# 13

## Constant Love

**Text:** "For I am sure that neither death, nor life, nor angels, nor principalities, nor things present, nor things to come, nor powers, nor height, nor depth, nor anything else in all creation, will be able to separate us from the love of God in Christ Jesus our Lord" (Rom. 8:38–39).

**Object:** Compass

**Theme:** We can depend on the love of God.

I have in my hand an object that is round, has four letters under a plate of glass—N, S, E, and W—and a needle that always points in the same direction. Can anyone tell me what I have? [Allow an opportunity for response.] Yes, that is correct. This is a compass.

Compasses are quite valuable instruments. Boy Scouts depend on them, ship navigators trust them, and airplane pilots rely on them. Why are compasses so valuable? [Allow adequate time for children to respond.] Compasses provide accurate information concerning direction, thus making it next to impossible to ever get lost. This information is provided by a tiny needle that always points in the same direction—north. No matter which way I turn, this way or this way, the needle continues to point north. This allows us to know the direction we are traveling no matter where we are going.

This compass reminds me of God's love. Like a needle that is constantly pointing in the same direction, God's love constantly points toward us. No matter which way we go, whatever we say or do, God always loves us. Even if our actions are wrong, God continues to love us. Like a compass that always points in the same direction, no matter which way we turn or wherever we go, God's love follows us all the days of our lives.

*Dear God, thank you for your constant love, and help us to love you in return. Amen.*

# 14

# Christian Hats?

**Text:** "'Come, O blessed of my Father, inherit the kingdom prepared for you from the foundation of the world; for I was hungry and you gave me food, I was thirsty and you gave me drink, I was a stranger and you welcomed me, I was naked and you clothed me, I was sick and you visited me, I was in prison and you came to me.' Then the righteous will answer him, 'Lord, when did we see thee hungry and feed thee, or thirsty and give thee drink? And when did we see thee a stranger and welcome thee, or naked and clothe thee? And when did we see thee sick or in prison and visit thee?' And the King will answer them, 'Truly, I say to you, as you did it to one of the least of these my brethren, you did it to me'" (Matt. 25:34–40).

**Object:** Fireman's hat, hard hat, and policeman's hat

**Theme:** Our commitment to Christ is demonstrated by Christian service to others.

If you were to see someone wearing a red hat like this one, you would probably guess that he or she is a _____ [fireman]. A yellow hat like this would indicate that the person is a _____ [construction worker]. And a blue hat like this is worn by a _____ [policeman]. In many cases we can readily identify the job a person has simply by looking at the hat he or she wears, such as we have done this morning.

The people in our church family have been called to perform a very special job. In fact, the reason we come to church is to prepare ourselves for this work. Yet if you look at our choir members, our ministers, or the congregation, you do not see anyone wearing a special hat to identify his or her job. But even though we do not wear special hats like firemen, construction workers, or policemen, our work is still of the greatest importance. You see, our job is that of Christian service. Each of us has made a commitment to Jesus Christ, and our job involves sharing the Good News of Christ. You may see Christian workers sharing the Good News of Christ in many different ways. Helping the poor, feeding the hungry, praying for those in need, lending a helping hand, and visiting the sick are just a few ways we share the love of Christ with others.

Come to think of it, Christians really do not need special hats. As Christians, we should be easily identified by the kind of lives we live.

*Dear God, help us to live in such a way that people will know we are Christians—through our love and our actions toward others. Amen.*

# 15

# A Perfect Copy

**Text:** "For those whom he foreknew he also predestined to be conformed to the image of his Son, in order that he might be the first-born among many brethren" (Rom. 8:29).

**Object:** Copier, black marker, and paper

**Theme:** We must be exact copies of Jesus.

This morning I have a rather large and heavy object with me. You can see that it plugs in and has several buttons to push. What do you suppose it is? [Allow adequate time for a response.] That's exactly right: this is a copying machine!

What is a copying machine? [Allow time for a response.] Of course, a copying machine makes copies! In fact, this copying machine will make an exact copy of almost anything you can write on a piece of paper.

Watch how a copier works. I am going to ask (name) _____ to write her name nice and big on this piece of paper so that everyone can see it. [When the child has completed this task, place the paper on the copier and ask another child to press the button that activates the copier.] (Name) _____, push this button, and let's see what happens!

Look! A piece of paper is coming out of the machine. Guess whose name is on it? Right, (name) _____'s! Is this the piece of paper (name) _____ wrote her name on? [Allow time for a response.] It sure looks like the same paper,

41

but it's not. Here is (name) _____'s sheet of paper. Both papers look exactly alike. No matter how hard we look, we cannot tell the difference. That is what makes a copier like this so great to have. We can always depend on it to turn out a copy that looks exactly like the original.

Did you know that there is someone we are supposed to copy in our Christian lives? Can anyone tell me who it is? [Allow children to respond.] Right! We are supposed to copy Jesus in everything we do—our talking, our actions, even what we feel, so that we are always trying our very, very best to be just like Jesus. The most wonderful thing about copying Jesus, trying to be exactly like him, is that everyone can always depend on us to act just like Jesus.

I am sure glad we have this machine that makes perfect copies. But I am even more glad when I see each of you trying your very best to be a perfect copy of Jesus.

*Dear God, help each of us to try to be a perfect copy of Jesus. Amen.*

# 16

# Key to Happiness

**Text:** "I will give you the keys of the kingdom of heaven, and whatever you bind on earth shall be bound in heaven, and whatever you loose on earth shall be loosed in heaven" (Matt. 16:19).

**Object:** Set of keys

**Theme:** The Bible provides the key for living a happy life.

The objects I have with me today should be very easy to recognize. [Show the objects, and allow the children to respond.] I am certain many of you began playing with keys like these at a very young age, perhaps even when you were just a little baby.

This set of keys is very important to me. I wonder if anyone might like to guess where some of these keys are used. [Allow the children to answer, and then follow with your response to each answer. For example, if a child says a lock on a door, you might respond, "Yes, this key opens the front door to my home," or if a child identifies a key to your car, you might respond, "Yes, this key will open my car door, and this key will start the engine."] So you can see how very important these keys are and how terribly upset I would be if they were lost.

There are also other types of keys, such as piano keys, desk drawer keys, and even keys for many of the new toys now being made. All keys of this sort are used either to

43

open or close a lock, such as on a door, or to start or turn off something, such as a car engine.

Sometimes the word *key* is used just to mean the "most important thing" or a "guide" like the key to success or the key to happiness. The Bible is really this sort of key, for it tells us many, many ways to live a happy and successful life. Jesus taught us that the single greatest key to happiness can be found in love.

I hope that whenever you see a set of keys, you will remember that even more important than having a set of keys like these is to have Jesus, who is our key to happiness.

*Dear God, thank you for giving us Jesus, who is the key to a happy life. Amen.*

# 17

# Molding Lives

**Text:** "Yet, O LORD, thou art our Father; we are the clay, and thou art our potter; we are all the work of thy hand" (Isa. 64:8).

**Object:** Ball of clay and clay figurine

**Theme:** We must allow the loving hands of God to shape and mold us.

I'm sure all of you have spent hours of enjoyment playing with a good ball of clay such as the one I have this morning. What are some of the objects you can make out of clay? [Children will provide a variety of answers.] I suppose with a good ball of clay you can create almost anything you want. All you have to do is roll and mold it into the desired shape.

I have with me a beautiful creation of _____ [figurine] made from a simple ball of clay similar to this one. Amazing as it may seem, something as pretty as this figurine can be created from a little ball of clay.

Let me share something with you far more amazing than this creation—what God can make out of you. Through the design of God's loving hands, he can shape you and mold you into children of true beauty. Much finer than the beauty of this simple figurine made from clay, God gives us beauty that enables us to live a life marked with kindness, peace, and love.

For God to be able to do this with you, I must let you in

on a little secret. God is able to shape and mold your life, only if you give him permission. You must put yourself into the loving hands of God, trusting him to carefully, tenderly, and lovingly mold you. If you are willing, you can become a beautiful creation shaped and molded by God.

Let's ask God to shape our lives.

*Dear God, take our lives and mold them, making them beautiful and useful to you. Amen.*

# 18

# Fruit of the Spirit

**Text:** "But the fruit of the Spirit is love, joy, peace, patience, kindness, goodness, faithfulness, gentleness, self-control; against such there is no law" (Gal. 5:22–23).

**Object:** Apple, orange, and peach

**Theme:** Christians produce identifiable fruits.

Can you tell the difference between an apple, peach, or orange tree? Since all of you are nodding your heads "yes," I suppose you feel that this is a rather simple task. How do you identify the difference between an apple, peach, or orange tree? By the shape of the leaves, by the texture of the bark, by the size of the tree, or _____? [Allow an opportunity for response.] Oh, I see. You say the easiest way to distinguish between the three trees is by the fruit each produces. A peach tree produces peaches, an apple tree produces apples, and an orange tree produces oranges. You have a good point, because trees not producing fruit are much more difficult to identify. But, of course, once the tree buds and little apples or oranges or peaches begin to grow, then it is simple to name the kind of tree.

The Bible teaches us that Christians also produce fruit. Some of the fruit of a Christian are love, courtesy, and kindness. Of course, these are not the kinds of fruit that you can eat like an apple, orange, or peach. Nevertheless, Christian fruit can easily be seen by the way we treat other people. In much the same way fruit grows on a tree, thus helping to identify the tree, Christian fruits of kindness, courtesy, and love help to identify each of us as followers of Jesus Christ.

Let's ask the Lord to help us grow the right kind of fruit.

*Dear God, help us to grow into healthy Christians, producing the fruits of kindness and love, as you have taught us. Amen.*

# 19

## Saltless Popcorn

**Text:** "You are the salt of the earth; but if salt has lost its taste, how shall its saltness be restored?" (Matt. 5:13a).

**Object:** Unsalted popcorn and saltshaker

**Theme:** As Christians we are the world's seasoning.

One of my favorite snacks has always been popcorn. I enjoy fixing popcorn at home, eating a box of popcorn at the movies, or munching on some during a party. In fact, I enjoy popcorn so much, I thought I might share some with you today. Do you all like popcorn? Good, I'm glad you do. I need a volunteer to taste this popcorn, just to make sure it is really as good as it looks. [Allow a child to come forward and taste the popcorn.] Tell me if that is not the best popcorn you have ever tasted! It isn't? Why, what's the matter? No salt? I forgot to shake on the salt. How could I have made such a mistake, forgetting something as important as salt on popcorn?

You know what? I just happen to have a saltshaker in my pocket. Let's see if a little salt will make the popcorn taste better. Yes, I agree with you; I do believe that is much better. Without the salt, this popcorn did not have much taste, but a little salt made a real improvement.

One time Jesus said, "You are the salt of the earth." Tasting this popcorn has helped me to understand what he meant. When we as Christians show our happiness and our love for other people, when we care for each other and are kind and forgiving, it is like adding salt to popcorn. Just like salt improves popcorn, we improve the lives of those around us. By our actions we can add flavor to life by making it better for everyone we meet.

*Dear God, teach us how to live so that we add flavor to life and help to bring happiness to others. Amen.*

# 20

# The Most Important Part

**Text:** "At that time the disciples came to Jesus, saying, 'Who
is the greatest in the kingdom of heaven?' And calling to
him a child, he put him in the midst of them, and said,
'Truly, I say to you, unless you turn and become like children, you will never enter the kingdom of heaven. Whoever humbles himself like this child, he is the greatest in
the kingdom of heaven'" (Matt. 18:1–4).

**Object:** Sparkplug

**Theme:** Every person is important.

I have brought a very small object with me to church today. Although this is not the kind of object you see every
day, I suppose some of you can tell me what it is. [Allow
adequate time for a response from the children.] That's exactly right. This is a sparkplug. Now perhaps you can tell
me where a sparkplug is used. [Children will probably respond with answers such as in a mini-bike, in a lawn
mower, or in a car.] This sparkplug is just a tiny part of my
car that helps make it run. My car also has a big engine, a
muffler, and other parts.

Boys and girls, I really wanted to bring the engine out of
my car and show you how important an engine is for making my car run. But it was much too heavy and too difficult
to get out of my car. So rather than lug in that big engine, I
brought this tiny sparkplug instead.

If I were to ask you which is the more important part of
a car, the engine or the sparkplug, what would you say?

[Different opinions may be offered at this point.] Both parts are very important, because the engine cannot work without the sparkplug and the sparkplug cannot work without the engine.

As silly as it may seem, sometimes people argue over who is the most important. Maybe you even know someone who believes he is more important than you. He may give silly reasons such as: I'm smarter than you, I live in a bigger house than you do, I have more toys than you have, I'm prettier or stronger than you, or I'm better because of the color of my skin.

No matter what reason a person may give for how important he or she is, Jesus taught that none of these things makes us important. In fact, Jesus taught that every one of us is important no matter what we do. Whether we perform small jobs like this sparkplug or large jobs like an engine, we are of equal importance in the eyes of God.

So next time you start wondering if someone is more important than you, remember the importance of this tiny sparkplug, and remember, too, that everyone is of equal importance to God.

*Dear God, help us to be humble and recognize the worth of all people. Help us to realize that each person is important to you. Amen.*

# 21

# Sharing a Load

**Text:** "Take my yoke upon you, and learn from me; for I am gentle and lowly in heart, and you will find rest for your souls. For my yoke is easy, and my burden is light" (Matt. 11:29–30).

**Object:** Ox yoke

**Theme:** Jesus shares every load in our lives.

Today I have an object I feel quite sure most of you have never seen. Can anyone tell me what this object is? [Several children may venture a guess, or perhaps some may have seen a yoke in a picture or in a movie.] This is called a yoke. How do you suppose it is used? [Allow children to respond.]

A yoke was made to fit around the neck of oxen, a type of cattle. A chain was hooked to the ring you see in the middle of the yoke. The other end of the chain was attached to a plow. The oxen would then pull the plow through the fields. Of course, most farmers today use tractors.

How many oxen do you think would wear this yoke? [Allow children to respond.] Yes, yokes were always made for two oxen. One ox would wear the yoke through this loop, and the other ox, standing right next to him, would wear the yoke through this loop. Why do you suppose a yoke was made for two oxen instead of just one? [Allow children to venture a guess; one answer should be close enough to continue.] Right! Many times a load would be much too heavy for one ox to pull, but two oxen pulling together would be strong enough to move a very heavy load.

In the Bible, Jesus asks us to accept his yoke. All of us carry loads or burdens throughout our lives. The kinds of loads we must carry are not exactly like the plows and wagons oxen pulled, but sometimes they feel just as heavy. A few of the loads we must pull as Christians include living as the good children God meant us to be—helping one another and loving everyone, even people who treat us unfairly.

Many times the loads we are asked to carry are just too much for us to pull alone. Like the yoke made for oxen, the yoke Christ offers us is made for two. In fact, Jesus never asks us to carry any burden in life without first promising his help. Jesus' promise is to be our special friend who will stand beside us and help us pull any load we may have to bear.

Let's thank God for giving us Jesus to help us carry whatever we may face in life.

*Dear God, thank you for giving us your Son Jesus to be yoked together with us and to be our Helper. Amen.*

## 22

# Directions for Living

**Text:** "Thomas said to him, 'Lord, we do not know where you are going; how can we know the way?' Jesus said to him, 'I am the way, and the truth, and the life; no one comes to the Father, but by me'" (John 14:5–6).

**Object:** Road map

**Theme:** The Bible provides guidance and direction for our lives.

We all look forward to the time of year when we can pack up the family car and travel to a favorite vacation spot, such as the beach, the mountains, or Grandmother's house. Suppose you were planning a trip for a few weeks this summer to Virginia Beach. Since Virginia Beach is far away, how would you go about finding the way to drive to the east coast? [Children should readily respond.] Yes, a map would be extremely helpful. Following a good map would make sure that you would indeed end up at Virginia Beach, not a beach in California or New York, or for that matter, anywhere else you did not want to go.

Just as maps guide us on trips, the Bible provides guidance for our lives. Jesus taught us that he is the way, the truth, and the life. What Jesus meant was that by following his guidelines, we can live happy, successful, and well-rounded lives. In fact, with Christ we need not worry about getting lost, since we will always be traveling in the right direction with him. All we need to do is follow the directions for our lives that are given to us in the Bible.

Let us thank God for giving us the Bible to show us the way through Jesus Christ.

*Dear God, thank you for the Bible and for the directions that Christ gave us for a happy life. Amen.*

# 23

# Playing Games

**Text:** "For whatever was written in former days was written for our instruction, that by steadfastness and by the encouragement of the scriptures we might have hope" (Rom. 15:4).

**Object:** Child's board game

**Theme:** For our lives to make sense, it is important to listen to the instructions of God.

This morning I have a brand-new game with me. There is nothing quite like the excitement of opening a new game. [As the children nod in agreement, open the game to disclose its contents.] I'm so excited about getting this new game, I can hardly wait to play it! There are so many different parts to this game! I wonder where they all belong? Come to think of it, I was so excited about getting this game that I nearly forgot that I do not even know how to play. Do any of you know how to play? Nobody? I wonder how we could learn to play? With all these different parts, this game looks pretty confusing. [Allow time for the children to respond. At least one child should suggest reading the rules of the game.] Reading the instructions is a great idea! I'm sure that knowing the rules will make this game a whole lot easier to play.

You are a smart group of boys and girls because you know the importance of reading and understanding the rules of this game before trying to play it. Did you know that rules are important not just with a game like this, but in our everyday lives? Our parents give us rules, too. They tell us to clean up our rooms, to be nice to our sisters and brothers, and to never play in the street. Our teachers also give us rules. They say we must raise our hands when we want to talk, and they tell us not to run in class and to always do our very best on our homework. Even God has given us some rules! He commands us to be kind to one another, to love one another, and to share with one another.

I am happy we have rules that help us to understand how to play this game. I'm sure that once we understand the rules, this game will be a lot of fun to play. But I am even happier we have the rules of our parents, our teachers, and God, because following them will help make our lives a lot more fun.

*Dear God, thank you for rules that teach us how to play games. But thank you even more for rules from you, our parents, and our teachers that help make our lives fun. Amen.*

# 24

# Magic Words

**Text:** "Love one another with brotherly affection; outdo one another in showing honor" (Rom. 12:10).

**Object:** Magic trick

**Theme:** Expressed kindness works like magic.

[Any magic trick may be done to begin this sermon. A simple yet effective trick I use is that of a disappearing coin. The trick is done by joining together the tips of your thumb, index, and middle fingers and placing a penny on top. Wave your other hand over the penny while reciting magic words. Pause momentarily over the penny and snap your fingers, hitting the coin with your middle finger and causing it to fly into your shirt or coat sleeve. When the coin disappears, the children will be amazed! By lowering your arm, the penny will drop into your hand. Reach over and pull a child's ear, and then open your hand to reveal the coin. Although this is an easy trick to perform, a little practice before performance is advised!]

I wonder how that penny got in (name) _____'s ear. The coin just disappeared from my thumb and then reappeared in his ear. Isn't that amazing? As amazing as my magic trick is, I know of something that is even more amazing than magic tricks: magic words!

Did you all know there are magic words? I am not talking about the magic word *alacazaam* that I used to make the coin disappear. I am talking about some magic words that we can use every day. Can anyone tell me which magic words I am talking about? [Allow the children to respond.] Of course, the magic words I am talking about are "please" and "thank you." Do you know why these words are magic? They are magic because of what happens when you say them. Tell me, what happens when you say "please" or "thank you"? [Allow the children time to respond.] Just watching how others smile and then treat us with kindness when we use these words shows us the amazing magic they have.

This week practice saying "please" and "thank you." Then watch carefully for the magic response of others.

*Dear God, thank you for magic words like "please" and "thank you." Help each of us to practice using these words every day.*

# 25

# The Master Piece

**Text:** "You call me Teacher and Lord; and you are right, for so I am" (John 13:13).

**Object:** Puzzle with an important piece

**Theme:** Our lives fit together properly when Jesus is kept at the center.

Putting a puzzle like this one together is a great way to spend a rainy day. Do you enjoy working puzzles? They can be a lot of fun, but some puzzles can be a little frustrating if they are hard to work.

The puzzle I have with me this morning looks like a hard one. Do any of you think you might be able to work it? [Allow a few children the opportunity to try. If the puzzle is not readily worked, suggest beginning with the piece of central importance. This will make their task easier.] I thought this was a difficult puzzle to work, but you all are smart enough to do it! (Name) _____ made working our puzzle a whole lot easier by beginning with this big piece in the middle. Once it was in place, (name) _____ and (name) _____ could see where the other pieces fit.

Watching you work this puzzle reminds me of something about each of our lives. Like this puzzle our lives are filled with lots and lots of different parts, like church and school and work and play. There are so many different parts to our lives, sometimes it is hard to know just how to put everything in place.

Just like this puzzle, we must begin putting our lives together with the most important part. That part is Jesus. If we put Jesus at the center of our lives, the other parts will fit together more easily.

Thank you for helping me work my puzzle this morning. You are all so smart. I hope you will always be smart enough to keep Jesus as the most important part of your lives.

*Dear God, help each of us to always be smart enough to keep Jesus as the most important part of our lives.*

# 26

# The Armor of Christ

**Text:** "Put on the whole armor of God, that you may be able to stand against the wiles of the devil" (Eph. 6:11).

**Object:** Protective vest

**Theme:** To wear the armor of Christ is to be safe in his love.

Perhaps you have seen a vest like this one on a person riding a bicycle. It is made from brightly colored cloth that glows in the dark. People who run or jog at night wear a vest like this, too. Have you seen one on people who are working on highway construction? Why do you think people wear this kind of clothing? [Allow the children to respond.] Of course, this vest provides protection. It helps prevent an accident when it might otherwise be difficult to see a person in traffic.

There are other kinds of clothing that protect. Firemen wear clothes that are fire-proof so that they will not catch on fire. Construction workers wear hard hats and shoes with thick soles. People who work with hot metal or who weld wear protective shields on their faces. Any time we are facing danger or harm we must be careful to be prepared.

A long time ago soldiers wore metal shields called armor. The apostle Paul explained how we could prepare ourselves to live as Christians. He said we must put on the whole armor of God so that we will be safe from evil. The armor of faith, the armor of strength, the armor of Christ's presence are sources of our protection.

It is good that we have bright vests that glow in the dark and fire-proof clothing and many kinds of hard hats and shields. But the best protection we can have for our day-to-day living is the Spirit of Christ dwelling in us and the sure knowledge that he is present with us at all times.

*Dear God, thank you for protecting us and loving us and especially for being with us at all times. Amen.*

# 27

# To Live as a Beacon

**Text:** "Let your light so shine before men, that they may see your good works and give glory to your Father who is in heaven" (Matt. 5:16).

**Object:** Beacon light or flashlight

**Theme:** We should live our lives as beacons of light in a dark world.

Many years ago lighthouses were built near the ocean. These were tall buildings that looked like towers. Each lighthouse had a strong light in the very top. This revolving beam of light could be seen from a long distance. I wonder if any of you know why these lighthouses were built with strong lights in them? [Allow the children to respond.] The light served as a beacon to guide ships safely into the harbor. The light that I have, as you can see, is large and strong and will glow for a long time. Some flashlights can serve as beacons, also, to light a path in the yard at night. When we are away from our homes at night, sometimes we leave a light in the window. When we come home, we see the light burning brightly, and we feel happy and safe.

Speaking of light and the way it brightens up the darkness reminds me of a Bible verse that describes a Christian as giving light to bring people to Christ. It says, "Let your light so shine before men . . . to give glory to your Father who is in heaven." If we live and act as Christ has taught us, we can be like beacons of light. We can show our happiness and our joy in being Christians, and other people will want to share the light of God's love.

*Dear God, help us to be like beacons of light in the world, showing others how to come to Christ. Amen.*

## 28

# A Tiny Seed in Good Soil

**Text:** "'The kingdom of heaven is like a grain of mustard seed . . .'" (Matt. 13:31).

**Object:** Mustard seeds

**Theme:** Planting seed in good soil will produce an abundant harvest.

I have some tiny objects with me this morning. I wonder if anyone knows what they are? [Allow time for responses.] These are mustard seeds. A mustard seed is perhaps one of the smallest seeds. As you can see, I can hold a large number in just a small space in my hand. Many seeds are tiny. Some flower seeds are so small you can hardly see them when you plant them in the ground. But then they sprout and grow into big plants with large, bright blooms.

Jesus talked about the tiny mustard seed. He said that if planted properly, the seed would grow into a large plant and eventually into a tree bigger than the other plants around it. Finally, large birds would be able to nest in it. Can you imagine one little seed making a plant that big? Jesus also said that if seeds were not planted in the right way, but were planted on rocky ground, they would not grow. If we want our flower seeds to grow and bloom or our mustard seeds to produce large plants, we cannot carelessly toss them out on just any ground. They must be planted in good, rich soil.

When Jesus was talking about planting seeds in good

soil, he was teaching us how to "plant" our lives in God's kingdom. He wants us to listen and understand God's Word, to accept God's presence in our lives, and to follow Christ's teachings. Even though our faith is small at first, we will grow as Christians and become as large as a tree in the kingdom of God.

*Dear God, thank you for the seeds that grow into plants and flowers. Help us to keep our lives centered in you so that we may grow strong and tall as Christian men and women.*

# 29

# Contents of the Bible

**Text:** "All scripture is inspired by God and profitable for teaching, for reproof, for correction, and for training in righteousness" (2 Tim. 3:16).

**Object:** Bible

**Theme:** The Bible contains instructions for Christian living.

I brought my favorite Bible to church today. I especially like the red leather binding and my name engraved on the front cover. This Bible is a very special book. Many books tell you how to repair a car or how to plant a garden or how to sew or how to decorate your home. Let's open my Bible and see what it contains. Well, first, it has several old church bulletins. And here is a pressed flower that I wore to a wedding. Here is an invitation to a graduation ceremony, a note to stop by my mother's home to pick up some food, and a newspaper clipping from several years ago.

All of these things that have been tucked in my Bible are not really what the Bible contains. There are wonderful words of wisdom, such as "Love one another" and "God is love." There are also wonderful teachings of Christ and instructions on how to live a happy life, such as "Do unto others as you would have them do unto you" and "Love your neighbor." Many people never know what marvelous advice and assurance are contained in the Bible. They often put it on a shelf where it collects dust, and they never open or study it. How much these people miss! I hope that you will learn to read your Bibles, that you will discover for yourselves the wisdom, the truth, and the instruction it contains for your lives.

*Dear God, thank you so much for giving us the Bible. Help us to read it and follow your teaching and instructions for our lives.*

# 30

# Following the Leader

**Text:** "And he said to them, 'Follow me, and I will make you fishers of men'" (Matt. 4:19).

**Object:** Baton

**Theme:** We should follow Christ as our supreme leader.

How many of you have seen a marching band? Have you noticed that all the people in the band play different kinds of musical instruments? They all start at the same time. They keep together as they march and play. And they all stop at the same time. That is because they have a leader who holds a baton similar to this one. The leader uses a baton to direct the band and to keep the tempo.

Can you imagine how a marching band would act if there were no leader? Each player would go in a different direction and play a tune all by himself. The players would start and stop at various times, never playing together. Isn't it a good thing that we have leaders who are trained to direct marching bands?

We also have leaders in our churches and our schools, people whom we can follow because they know how to lead us. We also have a supreme leader: Jesus has come to lead us into a happy and abundant life. He has asked us to accept him and to follow him that we might have meaningful lives. Some of us have promised to follow his leadership.

Occasionally we may lose our way because we follow

another leader or because we are not really paying attention, just as band players get out of line sometimes. But if we ask Jesus each day to guide us, if we follow his words from the Bible, he will lead us into happy, useful lives. There is no other leader with this power and no other way into eternal life.

*Dear God, thank you for being the Leader of our lives. May we accept you, love you, and follow your leading.*

# 31

## Erased Mistakes

**Text:** "Forbearing one another and, if one has a complaint against another, forgiving each other; as the Lord has forgiven you, so you also must forgive" (Col. 3:13).

**Object:** Chalkboard, eraser, chalk

**Theme:** God forgives our mistakes, and we should forgive others.

Most of you probably have a chalkboard like this at home. What are some of the ways you use a chalkboard? [Allow the children to respond.] Right! This board is great for playing office or school. Perhaps your mother has one in her kitchen to leave notes on or to write her grocery list or telephone numbers on. The nice thing about a chalkboard, or a blackboard, as it is sometimes called, is that it can be written on and then erased whenever you want. If you make a mistake when you are writing, you simply rub out or erase what you have written and start over again. Let's say I write _____ 's [Use the name of one of the children.] name on this board like this: _____ . [Misspell name.] Of course, that is not the way to spell (name) _____ . But, that's okay. All I have to do is erase with my eraser, and the mistake disappears.

As you have seen, to erase means to make something disappear or to blot out or rub out. This is exactly what happens when God forgives us for our mistakes. I do not mean mistakes in writing a name, but actions that are

73

wrong and hurt people. When we are sorry and ask God to forgive us, he just erases those bad deeds and allows us to start all over again.

We are taught to forgive others in the same way. If we have been mistreated or wronged by a friend, we should quickly forgive and forget and start anew, erasing the incident from our minds. Let's thank God for giving us a second chance.

*Dear God, we thank you for forgiveness and the fact that we can start anew. Help us to forgive others in the way that you forgive us.*

# 32

# The Master's Touch

**Text:** "I will praise the name of God with a song; I will magnify him with thanksgiving" (Ps. 69:30).

**Object:** Musical instrument

**Theme:** Jesus is the Master Teacher who can make our lives beautiful.

I wonder if anyone can tell me what kind of object I have with me this morning? Yes, you are right. This is a musical instrument. It is called a recorder. This particular recorder is nice and new, but did you know recorders much like this one existed in Bible times? Do you remember the stories about David the shepherd boy playing an instrument while watching over the sheep in the fields? Well, that instrument was a recorder much like the one I have here this morning!

Since this is such an important Bible musical instrument, I had thought I would play a nice song on this recorder for all of you to hear. But do you know something? Every time I tried to play a song nothing came out right. Do you know why? Because I do not know how to play this instrument. That is a problem, isn't it? What do you suppose could help? [Allow the children to make suggestions.] I think you all are exactly right. Having a teacher to help me learn to play this recorder is a great idea. Instead of just making noise, a teacher can help me to learn how to make a beautiful song with this instrument.

75

There is a man in our church who can make beautiful music come out of this recorder. I have asked (name) ———— to come and play a song for us. [Have someone play a song for you.] (Name) ————, did you have a teacher to help you learn how to play? You did. Do you think that I could learn to play like you if I had a teacher? I think you are right. A good teacher could help me learn to play this instrument beautifully just like you.

As important as it is to have a good teacher to help us learn how to play this instrument, it is even more important to have a good teacher to help us learn how to live a good life. The best Teacher who can help us learn how to live a good life is Jesus. From Jesus we can learn how to love our neighbors, how to treat others with kindness, and how to grow in the love of God.

Let's try every day to learn from Jesus to live as beautifully as (name) ———— can play this recorder.

*Dear God, help us each day to learn from our Teacher Jesus how to live a beautiful life. Amen.*

# 33

# Deep Roots in Christ

**Text:** "May your roots go down deep into the soil of God's marvelous love" (Eph. 3:17b, LB).

**Object:** Plant (small tree sapling) and scissors

**Theme:** We grow as Christians when we have deep roots in God's love.

I have a little tree that I want to transplant, or move to another place, in my yard. There is just one problem. I have only a little space in which to plant it, and I do not want it to grow very large. So I have to cut off part of it. [Cut the roots.] Now it will fit my space. I will dig a little hole, plant it, and water it every day, and it *will* grow, won't it. No? No roots? Do you think I have killed the plant by cutting off its roots? Can you tell me why a plant must have roots in order to live and grow? [Allow the children to make suggestions, and then continue.] The roots take up food and water from the soil. The better the root system, the better the plant will grow.

Our lives are like this plant. If we do not have deep roots in the Lord, if we are not planted firmly in his love, we will not grow and will wither because we are separated from the source of our spiritual nourishment. In his Letter to the Ephesians, the apostle Paul wrote, "May your roots go down deep in the soil of God's marvelous love." As we become deeply rooted, we begin to understand how high and

77

long and wide God's love really is, and we are filled and nourished by his love.

*Dear God, thank you for the great love you have given us in your Son Jesus Christ. Help us to accept your love, to have deep roots, so that we can grow into strong Christian men and women.*

# 34

# Reflecting God's Love

**Text:** "We can be mirrors that brightly reflect the glory of the Lord" (2 Cor. 3:18, LB).

**Object:** Hand mirror

**Theme:** A Christian reflects the spirit of Christ living within.

The mirror that I have with me today is just a small hand mirror, but, as you know, there are many kinds of mirrors. You probably have one in your room at home. Have you practiced making faces in front of it? If you smile, what kind of face do you see in the mirror? [A smile.] If you frown, what kind of face do you see in the mirror? [A frown.] A mirror reflects, or gives back to you, a true image. There are all types of mirrors—round and square and oval, large wall mirrors and gold-framed mirrors. Many are used to reflect light to make a room more attractive.

A Christian is very much like a mirror, reflecting the loving spirit of Christ. As we find new life in Christ, as we allow him to mold our lives, other people can see his light shining from us. Jesus wants us to let our light shine before men that we may glorify the Father (Matt. 5:16). If we are to be mirrors that reflect Christ's image, we want to be the best possible mirrors that we can be and shine as brightly as we can. Let us ask God to help us.

*Dear God, we want to shine as lights in the world. We want to be like mirrors, reflecting your Spirit within us. Help us to work and pray to become your images.*

# 35

## More Than Bread

**Text:** "And he humbled you and let you hunger and fed you with manna, which you did not know, nor did your fathers know; that he might make you know that man does not live by bread alone, but that man lives by everything that proceeds out of the mouth of the LORD" (Deut. 8:3).

**Object:** Loaf of bread

**Theme:** Through God we can experience life in all its fullness.

This morning I have something with me I am sure you see and eat almost every day. What are some of your favorite ways to eat bread? [Suggestions will probably include peanut butter and jelly sandwiches, french toast, and toast for breakfast.]

Suppose I told each of you that starting today all you could eat was bread. For breakfast I would give you one piece of bread, for lunch I would give you one piece of bread, and then for dinner I would give you maybe two pieces of bread. Would you like having bread for breakfast, lunch, and dinner with nothing else at all? No more salad or meat or vegetables, or even dessert—just bread! [By this point, the children will respond by shaking their heads and talking about how awful this would be.] Eating bread and nothing else would be awful. In fact, before long I bet you would be pretty sick and tired of bread.

Eating bread alone and nothing else reminds me of

what it is like to live without God. Living without God in your life is like eating only bread. Before long we get sick of life and tired of everything. When we live with God, it is like enjoying salad and meat and vegetables and dessert along with our bread. With God we can enjoy so much more in life because he shares life with us.

Let's thank God today, not just for bread, but for all the wonderful foods that go with it. Let's thank God, too, not just for life, but for his willingness to share it with us.

*Dear God, thank you for making life more enjoyable by sharing it with us.*

# 36

# Let's Have a Party!
## (New Year's Day)

**Text:** "This is the day which the LORD has made; let us rejoice and be glad in it" (Ps. 118:24).

**Object:** New Year's whistle for each child

**Theme:** We should celebrate the gift of each new year God gives to us.

It is hard to believe, but 19_ _ is almost over. We will soon begin a brand-new year. Can anyone tell me what year will come next?

Starting a new year is always exciting. Grown-ups usually do some pretty silly things to celebrate the coming of a new year. One of the silliest things they do is to go to parties and stand around blowing little whistles like these. [Demonstrate.]

I wonder why there is so much excitement over starting a new year? [Allow time for the children to respond. At least one child should suggest that the excitement surrounds the celebration of another year of life.] Of course, beginning a new year is a great reason to get excited. Just think, in the year to come, all of you will continue to grow, everyone will have a birthday, there will be more opportunities to learn in school and church, and there will be wonderful trips to visit grandparents. No wonder there is so much excitement over the beginning of a new year: there are many wonderful things to do!

In all this excitement, it is important for us to remember who gives us this new year and who gives us life. Can anyone tell me? [Allow the children to respond.] Right! God gives life to all of us and everything around us—the flowers, birds, pets—everything. Just knowing how much God has given to us is a great reason to celebrate and have a party.

This week I hope all of you will remember how much God has given to you. Then blow your whistle just to let God know how excited you are about starting a brand-new year.

*Dear God, thank you for the gift of a brand-new year. Help us to remember as we celebrate that all of life is a gift from you.*

# 37

# The Weakest Link
## (Winter)

**Text:** "So we, though many, are one body in Christ, and individually members one of another" (Rom. 12:5).

**Object:** Snow-tire chains

**Theme:** The church is only as strong as its individual members.

Something wonderful happened this past week. [This lesson must follow a good snow. The children will immediately begin talking about the newly fallen snow.] Can you tell me what you did in the snow? [Answers should include building snowmen and forts, making snow angels, etc.] Snow can be a lot of fun!

Did you have to go anywhere in the car? As much fun as snow can be, it can present quite a bit of difficulty in driving a car. Unless your mother or father has a special car made to go in snow, the tires of your family car will probably spin and spin, and you will go nowhere at all. To solve this problem maybe your parents have a set of these. Does anyone know what these are? [Allow the children to respond.] Yes, these are tire chains to use in the snow. Each chain wraps around the rear tire of a car and then fastens like this. When the tire turns, the chains dig deep into the snow, allowing the car to go almost anywhere.

As nice as these chains have been in helping me drive my car, I have had a problem with them. Every once in a while one tiny link of the chain breaks. Now you would not think this would cause much of a problem since there are over two hundred links on each tire chain. But let me assure you, if even one link breaks, I have a real problem. In fact, when only one link breaks, I am no longer able to use this chain until it is fixed. Although every other link may be strong and is working as hard as it can, all the good links cannot make up for the one link that breaks.

There is an old saying, "A chain is only as good as its weakest link." This means that no matter how strong a chain may be, if one link is weak and breaks, the whole chain is ruined. This saying is not only true about chains, but also about a church. No matter how strong a church may be, it can only be as good as the people who belong to it. For this reason, it is very important that every person does his or her very best. If just one person does not try, then the whole church is weakened.

Each of you can help by giving your very best. Come to church regularly. Be ready to listen and learn what God wants for you. Make yourself strong, and you will do your part to make the church strong.

*Dear God, thank you for our church and the people who work to make it strong. Help all of us to do our part. Amen.*

# 38

## Pure as Snow
### *(Winter)*

**Text:** "Come now, let us reason together, says the LORD: though your sins are like scarlet, they shall be as white as snow" (Isa. 1:18).

**Object:** Large bowl of snow

**Theme:** God cleanses and purifies our lives.

Something wonderful happened last _____ . Does anyone remember? Of course—we had a beautiful white snowfall.

Playing in the snow can be a lot of fun. Snow provides many opportunities for games, creativity, and adventure. What sort of fun did you have in the snow this week? [Typical answers will include building snowmen, sledding, constructing forts, making snow ice cream, etc.]

Snow comes at such a wonderful time. Just when everything looks so lifeless—the ground is dark and drab, the trees are bare, hardly anyone plays outdoors—suddenly everything is changed by a glistening, pure, white snowfall. The trees and the ground are given new life, and none of us can resist going out once again to play.

When Jesus enters our hearts, he changes our dark, drab lives into clean, pure lives—as clean and pure as a newly fallen snow. Even better than a snow that may fall only a few times during the year, Jesus will restore our lives to purity and cleanliness any day of the year. Even when we make a real mess of things—for example, being mean to a friend, refusing to help someone in need, or self-ishly refusing to let others play with our toys—God can still change each of our muddied lives back to pure lives—as pure as this snow—if we only ask his forgiveness.

Next time you are watching a new snowfall, think of new beginnings. New beginnings are given to each of us when we ask God to make our lives as pure as the newly fallen snow.

*Thank you, Lord, for purifying our lives like new snow and changing our darkness to light. Amen.*

# 39

# Flowers for Mother
## (Mother's Day)

**Text:** "Train up a child in the way he should go, and when he is old he will not depart from it" (Prov. 22:6).

**Object:** Potted flowers

**Theme:** We need to express thankfulness for mothers who nurture us.

Can anyone tell me what day it is? That's right—today is Mother's Day.

I'm not sure who planned it, but putting Mother's Day in the spring was really very smart. Spring is the time for flowers to bloom, flowers we can appreciate all summer long. Spring is also a good time to remember how much we love and appreciate our mothers.

Growing a beautiful flower like this one takes a lot of time and care. What do flowers need in order to grow? [Children will volunteer such answers as sunshine, rich soil, rain, protection from plant-eating animals, and so on.]

Flowers are a lot like people. If we are to grow, we need a lot of care, like a flower receives. That is where mothers come in. Mothers are especially good at caring for us and helping us to grow up in the right way. What are some of the ways your mother helps you grow? [Allow children adequate time to respond, and then summarize.] A mother's love is like sunshine, and her teaching is like rich soil. She corrects and guides us, and her protection keeps us safe.

I hope you will take time today to tell your mother how very much you love her. As we have done this morning, you might even explain why spring flowers remind you of her care.

*Dear God, how can we ever thank you enough for mothers who do so many things for us? Help us to show our love for them today and every day. Amen.*

# 40

## Gone Fishing
### (Spring/Summer)

**Text:** "And Jesus said to them, 'Follow me and I will make you become fishers of men'" (Mark 1:17).

**Object:** Fishing pole

**Theme:** We are to follow Jesus' example and become fishers of people.

Now that it is summer there are many wonderful things we can do outdoors. Many people love to go fishing. How many of you have ever been fishing? [Allow children to respond. You may even hear a story or two!] I see that several of you have been fishing. [Hold up the fishing pole.] Maybe you can tell me what this is. Yes, this is a fishing pole. How do you use a fishing pole? [Allow children to explain.] You mean, if I let out my line [demonstrating] like this—assuming, of course, that there is water out there and not carpet—before long a great big fish may come along and get caught on my hook? Have any of you actually caught a fish? Fishing is a lot of fun and a great way to spend a hot summer day.

Did you know that Jesus once said that he wants us to be fishermen? But he was not talking about catching fish; he was talking about catching people. Do you think that Jesus meant that we should try to catch people with a fishing pole? No. The way to catch people, Jesus said, is by sharing the love of God with them.

Spending a day catching fish is a lot of fun. But spending a day catching people is even more fun. Make sure you spend some time every day sharing the special love of God. Then you can be a fisher of people.

*Dear God, help us every day to be fishers of people by sharing your special love.*

# 41

# Some Explosion!
## (Independence Day)

**Text:** "Beware of practicing your piety before men in order to be seen by them; for then you will have no reward from your Father who is in heaven" (Matt. 6:1).

**Object:** Empty firecracker (Cover an empty toilet tissue roll with aluminum foil and insert a wick at one end.)

**Theme:** We can look good on the outside and still be empty on the inside.

Instead of sitting nice and close like we usually do during the children's sermon, I am going to ask you all to stand about ten feet away. I am very excited about the object I have with me this morning. Can anyone tell me what this is? Exactly! This is a giant firecracker. I am excited because I believe that I am the first person ever to think of lighting a firecracker in church. Isn't this a great idea? [The children will probably be too amazed to even respond.] Let's turn the lights down in our sanctuary to make sure we can see all of the fireworks when our firecracker explodes. [Light the firecracker.] You may want to cover your ears. A giant firecracker like this can be pretty loud. [Keep talking about your expectations for this firecracker until the wick fizzles out.]

What happened? Nothing, nothing at all! I do not understand. Come on over and let's take a closer look. This is such a beautiful firecracker. I cannot believe it did not work. What do you suppose the problem might be? [Allow some time for suggestions. At least one child should suggest investigating the problem by looking inside the firecracker.]

No wonder our firecracker did not work! Look inside! It is empty. Can you believe it? I thought this was going to be a great firecracker just because it looked perfect on the outside. I forgot that it is what is on the inside that really counts. What a sad mistake to make.

Today has reminded me of another mistake we often make. That is the mistake of thinking that if we look good enough on the outside, what is on the inside does not really matter. In other words, we might think that if our hair looks nice or that if we have pretty clothes, then that is all that matters. But that is a sad mistake to make, because what is most important is not what we have on the outside, but who we are on the inside. Unless we have love, joy, and friendliness in our hearts, we can be as empty on the inside as this firecracker, no matter how good we look on the outside.

Let's ask God to help us remember that looking good on the outside is not as important as what is on the inside.

*Dear God, help each of us to always remember that what is on the inside is more important than looking good on the outside.*

# 42

# Broken Strings
## (Summer)

**Text:** "Therefore, if any one is in Christ, he is a new creation; the old has passed away, behold, the new has come" (2 Cor. 5:17).

**Object:** Tennis racket with several broken strings

**Theme:** God can repair the broken parts of our lives.

As you came to church this morning I am sure you could not help but notice what a beautiful day this is. All of you will have a great time playing outside this afternoon. As soon as church is over, I am going to play outside, too. I love tennis, and today is a perfect day to play. I even brought my tennis racket with me this morning so that I can play as soon as possible right after church.

Oh, no! Look at this racket! Look at what has happened! Do you think I can play with this racket? Why not? [The children will quickly point out the difficulty of playing with a tennis racket that has broken strings.] You are right! I would not stand a chance of winning with this racket. In fact, with all these broken strings I doubt if I could play at all.

Do you think I could have this racket fixed, or should I just throw it away? [The children will probably be divided on this question.] There really is no need to throw this racket away, because it can be fixed. I can take this racket to a sports shop and have these broken strings replaced

95

with brand-new strings. Once the new strings are in place, this racket will be like new again.

Knowing how this racket can be fixed reminds me of how God works in each of our lives. Have you ever done something you knew you were not supposed to do? [The children may provide some examples at this point.] Hitting our brothers and sisters, saying something mean to our moms or dads, or mistreating friends can make us feel about as worthless as tennis rackets with broken strings. No matter how bad we feel, we should always remember we can be fixed. God can take the worst parts of us and make us like brand-new.

I am happy that this racket can be made like new again. But I am even happier that God can make us like new.

*Dear God, thank you for fixing us when we are broken and making us feel like brand-new.*

# 43

## Keeping Warm
### (Autumn)

**Text:** "You shall walk in all the way which the LORD your God has commanded you, that you may live, and that it may go well with you" (Deut. 5:33a).

**Object:** Quilt or afghan with an obvious pattern or design

**Theme:** God loves us so much that he has made beautiful designs for our lives.

Have you noticed how cold the nights are lately? Why do you suppose the nights are becoming colder and colder? [Allow adequate time for the children to point out that winter is coming.] That is exactly right. Winter is just around the corner.

With the coming of winter, your mommy or daddy will probably reach up into the closet and get an extra blanket to put on your bed. Why do you need another blanket on your bed? [Allow adequate time for a child to explain that an extra blanket will keep him or her warm on cold nights.]

As you can see, this morning I have a blanket with me. This is no ordinary blanket. In fact, this happens to be my favorite blanket. A good friend of mine spent many hours making this blanket for me. If you look closely, you will see a beautiful design. The most wonderful thing about this design is that it fits together to make this whole blanket.

When it gets cold at night, I use this blanket to stay nice

and warm. [You may want to drape the blanket around you to illustrate your point.] Once I am warm, I cannot help but remember how much I was loved by the person who made this blanket for me.

Even greater than the love of the person who made this blanket for me, is God's love for each of us. God loves us so much that he has made a beautiful design for our lives. The most wonderful thing about God's design is that it all fits together. Whenever I feel cold, lonely, or maybe even a little sad on the inside, just knowing God loves me and has a design for me can make me feel warm and happy again.

*Dear God, thank you for the beautiful design you have for our lives. Amen.*

# 44

## Falling Leaves
### (Autumn)

**Text:** "Therefore, if any one is in Christ, he is a new creation; the old has passed away, behold, the new has come" (2 Cor. 5:17).

**Object:** Colorful fall leaves

**Theme:** God gives the promise of new life to us.

Everywhere we look lately, beautiful leaves of many different colors are beginning to fall. These leaves have been in the trees all summer. Why do you suppose they are falling now? [Children will respond with a variety of answers.] You say that it is fall and that is the time of year for leaves to fall off the trees. Does that mean the trees are dying? No, the trees are not really dying, they are just getting rid of their old, worn-out leaves. The trees will then go to sleep for the winter. About six months from now, in the early spring, the trees will wake up and sprout brand-new leaves.

When Jesus enters our hearts, it is like getting rid of old, worn-out leaves. We shed old habits, bad attitudes, and selfish ways. Like a tree that finds new life in the warmth of spring, God promises to each of us new life through the warmth of his love. We can then begin to grow and mature in the sunshine of his care.

Let's thank God for the opportunity to shed old lives and be born anew into life with him.

*Dear God, thank you that we can find new life in your Son Jesus Christ. Help us to grow to be more like him. Amen.*

100

# 45

# Planting and Reaping
## (Autumn)

**Text:** "Do not be deceived; God is not mocked, for whatever a man sows, that he will also reap" (Gal. 6:7).

**Object:** Tulip bulbs

**Theme:** When planted, seeds of character will grow, mature, and multiply in our lives.

I want you to pass these objects around. Take some time to touch them and look at them closely before you try to tell me what they are. [Pass out several tulip bulbs, and allow adequate time for a response.]

These objects are tulip bulbs. This is the time of the year when we plant bulbs. Bulbs like this one will sleep underground until early spring when they will be awakened by the warm ground. Then they will push their way out of the ground and blossom into beautiful tulips.

Do you suppose I could get petunias if I plant these bulbs? I like petunias better than tulips. Maybe if I wish hard enough, petunias will grow when spring comes. No? Why not? You mean I have to plant petunias if I want petunias to grow? That does make good sense. Planting tulips and hoping to see petunias grow in the spring is pretty foolish. Can you imagine planting weeds, hoping for good things to eat like corn, beans, carrots, and tomatoes? You would, of course, end up with weeds and nothing at all to eat. If I want tomatoes or corn to grow, I need to plant tomatoes or corn. Planting the right kind of seeds is very important to get the results you want.

The Bible teaches us that whatever we sow, we will also reap. In other words, whatever we plant we will get back. If we plant seeds of happiness, we will find happiness as we go through life. If we plant seeds of kindness, we will find _____ [kindess] as we go through life. If we plant seeds of understanding, we will find _____ [understanding] as we go through life. If we plant seeds of love, we will find _____ [love] as we go through life.

Let's ask God to help us plant the right kinds of seeds.

*Dear God, help us to plant the right kinds of seeds so that, in return, we will reap kindness, understanding, and love. Amen.*

# 46

## Wearing a Mask
### *(Halloween)*

**Text:** "What is man that thou art mindful of him, and the son of man that thou dost care for him? Yet thou hast made him little less than God, and dost crown him with glory and honor" (Ps. 8:4–5).

**Object:** Halloween mask

**Theme:** We must let others see us as we really are.

[Begin this sermon by putting on a Halloween mask.] Why are you looking at me so funny and giggling? Oh, you think my mask is funny! Well, I thought I would go ahead and wear my mask so I would be sure to be ready for Halloween.

Are you all going to trick or treat on Halloween night? Why are you going? Are you going to dress up? What are you going to be? [Allow time for the children to respond to each of these questions.] It is fun to dress up like a clown or a monster or a cartoon character. Some of you might have such great costumes that nobody will even know who you are!

[Take the mask off.] Wearing a mask on Halloween is lots of fun. What do you think would happen if you decided you did not want to take off your mask after Halloween? Let's say you came home on Halloween night and told your mom and dad, "I think I'll just wear this mask to bed." And then the next day you left your mask on to go to school and to the store. Do you think your family or your friends would like it if you kept your mask on every single day? [Allow the children to respond.] I think you are right. Your family and friends would not like that very much. Before long they would want to see the real you again.

As much fun as it is to wear a Halloween mask, the best part of you is the part that is real. The real you—how you look, how you act, and how you feel—is what is so special to your family, your friends, and God. Always remember, except when you trick or treat, let others see the real you.

*Dear God, thank you for making each of us special. Thank you for parents and friends who love us just the way we are.*

# 47

## The Greatest Gift
### (Thanksgiving)

**Text:** "The LORD God formed man of dust from the ground, and breathed into his nostrils the breath of life; and man became a living being" (Gen. 2:7).

**Object:** Baby

**Theme:** God's greatest gift to us is life.

This week is a very important one, a week when you are sure to get lots and lots of great food to eat. Soon your stomachs will be full of turkey, dressing, cranberries, sweet potatoes, rolls, and much more.

Why will your family be eating all this great food? That's right, this week we are celebrating Thanksgiving. Why do we celebrate Thanksgiving? [Children will probably respond with a brief history of Thanksgiving, pointing out how thankful the Pilgrims were that they survived a difficult winter. At this point, ask the children to express some of the things for which they are especially thankful. Answers will probably include their mothers, fathers, sisters, brothers, friends, flowers, homes, food, and so on. Feel free to suggest some yourself.] I suppose we could talk all day about the many things for which we are thankful. God has given all of us so much.

During this Thanksgiving season, as you are eating your turkey and munching those delicious cranberries, I would like you to remember the greatest gift given to us by God.

This little baby, with its smile, cries, wiggling fingers and toes, has God's greatest gift—the gift of life. In fact, all of us have been given this very special gift. The gift of life is something for which we should always be thankful. We should thank God for the gift of life not only on Thanksgiving Day, but every day of our lives. Let's thank God right now for this very special gift.

*Dear God, thank you for giving us life so that we can know all the joys of having family, friends, and your Son Jesus Christ. Amen.*

# 48

# What Can I Give?
## *(Christmas)*

**Text:** "I appeal to you therefore, brethren, by the mercies of God, to present your bodies as a living sacrifice, holy and acceptable to God, which is your spiritual worship" (Rom. 12:1).

**Object:** Several gift packages and bag of small bows

**Theme:** The most valuable gift we can give to God is ourselves.

This is a time for giving gifts. I have gifts for my wife, for my children, for some of my friends, and for my parents. Why do we give gifts at Christmas? [Allow children adequate time to respond.] Right! To show that we love someone. Or sometimes to say "thank you." But mostly to show our love. Did you know that we celebrate Christmas because God loved us so much that he gave the greatest gift of all—Jesus Christ? In fact, on Christmas we are really celebrating Jesus' birthday.

While you have been deciding on the gifts you want to give to people you love, have you thought about how you will show your love to God? If you were asked to bring the one thing you like most to God, what would you bring? Your favorite toy? Some jewelry? Did you know that you have a gift for God far more valuable than toys and jewelry? That gift is yourself. Giving yourself would please God more than any gift you could buy. In return for God's gift of his Son, he only asks that we give ourselves to him—our time, our talents, and our money.

So that you can remember that the most precious gift we can give to God is ourselves, I have a bow for each of you to wear today. As you wear your bow, remember: The best gift you can give to God is yourself.

*Dear God, thank you for the gift of your Son Jesus Christ. Help us to show our love for you by giving ourselves in serving you and by sharing what we have with others. Amen.*

# 49

## Good News
### (Christmas)

**Text:** "And the angel said to them, 'Be not afraid; for behold, I bring you good news of a great joy which will come to all the people'" (Luke 2:10).

**Object:** Telegram

**Theme:** The best way to share the good news of Jesus Christ is to tell others about his great love.

How many of you have ever received a telegram? A telegram is a message sent by wire. It can be sent very quickly, perhaps in an hour or two, to almost any part of the world. It would require several days for a letter to reach the same place. A telegram may say, "Happy Birthday" or "Happy Anniversary." Sometimes, even money is wired or telegraphed to another person. A telegram may be sent to inform someone of the time of arrival on an airplane. Many times a telegram will say, "Good news, our baby boy [or girl] was born today."

When the angel announced the birth of Jesus to the shepherds in the fields, he said, "Be not afraid; for behold, I bring you good news of a great joy which will come to all the people." This was certainly the greatest news anyone has ever received.

A telegram is just one way of sharing good news. We may also use the telephone or write letters. The best way to share the Good News of Jesus Christ is to live the way he has taught us, and to tell others about his wonderful love.

*Dear God, thank you for the many ways we can announce good news to our family and friends. Above all, help us to share the Good News of Christ's love to all people. Amen.*

# 50

# Whose Birthday?
## (Christmas)

**Text:** "For to you is born this day in the city of David a Savior, who is Christ the Lord" (Luke 2:11).

**Object:** Birthday cake

**Theme:** Christmas is a celebration of Jesus' birthday.

I am sure all of you are getting ready for a really great Christmas. This is such an exciting time of year! Everywhere we look we see things that remind us that Christmas is almost here. What are some of the things you have seen that tell you Christmas is just around the corner? [Children should quickly respond with stories about seeing Santa, decorating a Christmas tree, wrapping presents, etc.]

The special things we do during the Christmas season are so much fun: making decorations, wrapping gifts, talking to Santa. But the real reason we are so happy and have so much fun during this season is because we are celebrating a very special birthday. Whose birthday is on Christmas Day? Of course, Christmas is Jesus' birthday. On Christmas Day we are having a big party to celebrate Jesus' birthday.

What is so special about Jesus' birthday? [Allow children to respond. At least one child should point out that Jesus is God's gift to each of us.] Yes, during Christmas we remember God's greatest gift of love when he gave us his Son Jesus.

The best way to celebrate a birthday is with a birthday cake. This birthday cake is for Jesus. As you eat this cake, I want you to remember baby Jesus, whose birthday we are celebrating this Christmas season.

*Dear God, thank you for sending us baby Jesus on Christmas Day. May we celebrate his birthday, remembering that he is your greatest gift of love to each of us.*